A Christian Response to Crisis

Book 2 of the
Christian Response Series

Dr. Stan E. DeKoven

A Christian Response to Crisis

Book 2 of the
Christian Response Series

Dr. Stan E. DeKoven

Copyright © 2012 By Stan E. DeKoven, Ph.D.

ISBN 978-1-61529-030-7

Published by:

Vision Publishing
1672 Main Street, E109
Ramona, CA
www.booksbyvision.com

1-800-9-VISION

Printed In the United States of America

All scripture references are taken from the New American Standard Bible and used by permission

Table of Contents

Introduction

How is a Christian leader or person in general respond to a crisis? When trouble comes as it always does, how are we to react as effective caregivers in the communities where we live? In this booklet, which is a part of our "Christian Response Series," we discuss the most important points of helping to solve a crisis. When crisis comes, how can we help in an effective and clearly biblical fashion?

Most of the material found in this booklet is taken from the more exhaustive work done by this author in the text, Crisis Counseling. For those studying for a ministry in counseling or for lay and pastoral leaders desiring to be better equipped for ministry to counseling needs, this work is highly recommended.

Before exploring key responses to counseling that are helpful, let us look at the common response found in churches when a crisis comes to the church.

(1) The Ostrich Approach

Bury it and hide. Pretend that it didn't happen. Think of the harm that could come if anyone found out. A former colleague of mine once told me of a certain pastor's fears of exposing problems in the church. He likened it to picking up of a rock. When you do so, the bugs start crawling out! It is better to keep the rock where it is (and the inherent church problems) than to expose people's problems, for fear of the repercussions. Let's not let anyone else know.

We don't want to hurt anyone. As one might imagine, running or hiding from a crisis will often simply make it worse.

(2) The Cancer Approach

If a problem is seen as truly too grievous to deal with (such as child abuse, an affair in leadership, etc.) perhaps it is best to just "cut the person off" as if they have cancer, and that will solve the problem. Well, it may solve one problem (the negative ramifications to others) but is it really a Christian response?

(3) The Healing Community

The church is not exempt from the manifestation of sin. Problems do occur; crisis of all different kinds may come. Regardless the cause of a crisis, the people involved need proper care and nurture if they and the communities we live in will see something good come from something ill.

When crisis comes, first we must confront the situation head on. We must know the facts as best we can. Yet we must do so with an open mind.

Second, we must if possible, talk with the responsible parties; offering comfort and support motivated by love. Although Jesus never excused sin or the sinner, he was willing to love and pardon. Each individual needs to be heard and offered a clear opportunity for restoration through repentance.

Third, keep all communication confidential and where necessary, squelch rumors and gossip. There is a natural human tendency to want to know all the details.

Fourth, offer continued ministry from the church so that continued restoration might occur. Whatever we do, when one of our own is wounded even if it is self- inflicted, we must be willing and able to bind up their wounds and allow healing to occur. We must not shoot our wounded.

Most of our churches today are ill prepared to handle the crisis that will inevitably happen within the family, and the family of God. Few churches have trained laity or pastoral staff who can help in times of real crisis. Yet it is precisely there, between the rock and the hard place that the love of Christ is carefully and judiciously applied. It is there that it can most fully and completely "heal the broken hearted and set the captive free."

Jesus stated;

[34] *"Then the King will say to those on His right, 'Come, you who are blessed of My Father, inherit the kingdom prepared for you from the foundation of the world.* [35] *For I was hungry, and you gave Me something to eat; I was thirsty, and you gave Me something to drink; I was a stranger, and you invited Me in;* [36] *naked, and you clothed Me; I was sick, and you visited Me; I was in prison, and you came to Me.'* [37] *Then the righteous will answer Him, 'Lord, when did we see You hungry, and feed You, or thirsty, and give You something to drink?* [38] *And when did we see You a stranger, and invite You in, or naked, and clothe You?* [39] *When did we see You sick, or in prison, and come to You?'* [40] *The King will answer and say to them, 'Truly I say to*

you, to the extent that you did it to one of these brothers of Mine, even the least of them, you did it to Me"

(Mt 25:34-40NASB)

Within the remainder of this booklet, it is hoped that you will uncover the dynamics which can cause such distress and breakdown; while gaining an understanding of how to effectively and judiciously provide care for the walking wounded that live within our church and community.

Crisis Defined

What is crisis?

Webster's Definition: "A turning point in anything; decisive or crucial time, stage or event; a time of great danger or trouble, whose outcome decides whether possible bad consequences will follow."

A crisis is an event, whether a "normal" part of our developmental life or "accident", which temporarily changes our world and necessitates an emotional/spiritual adjustment.

Crises are not of themselves good or bad. Their impact is determined by the meaning one gives to the event, and the feelings generated. The impact is often determined by;

1) The closeness of the event
2) Perception of the meaning of the event

In either case, a crisis definitely makes us stop and evaluate, seek the Lord, and make the necessary adjustments to cope effectively.

Phases of a Crisis

H. Norman Wright, in his book **Crisis Counseling: Helping People in Crisis and Stress** (Here's Life

Publications 1985), outlines the four primary phases of crisis. They are:

1) Impact
2) Withdrawal Confusion
3) Adjustment
4) Reconstruction/Reconciliation

Most of us have experienced a crisis of some proportion during our lifetime, forcing us to make a life adjustment. Knowing what a crisis is and how to manage it is of vital importance in the ministry to one another in the body of Christ. Let us begin our study by looking in great detail at the four phases of crisis.

Crisis Counseling in Everyday Lives

The Four Phases of Crisis

I.   Impact

Our initial response to any given crisis, whether it is developmental such as the birth of a new child, a change in a career, a new teenager in the family; or situational, such as an accident, loss of a job, separation, divorce, or death is determined by the impact that the event has upon us and the meaning that we give it. For some people, the smallest situations can create great anxiety, sadness or depression. How we respond depends on many factors including:

1. Our genetic predisposition toward stress.
2. Our present spiritual walk.
3. Our understanding of the things of God as it is outlined within the word of God.
4. Our support systems, such as family and friendships existing both within and outside of the body of Christ.
5. Our history in regards to the management of crisis situations in our families.

Needless to say, the impact of a crisis cannot be fully understood until the crisis occurs. We should learn love and tolerance for one another, especially in the midst of a crisis event.

II.   Withdrawal/Confusion

Normally when a crisis comes, it is difficult for us to understand fully why this could have happened to us. When someone loses a loved one, a job, or has some other major change occur in their life, there can be times of withdrawal or confusion that can be virtually immobilizing. It is at those times that people need great support and loving, gentle encouragement to assist them in working through the crisis.

III. Adjustment

Because a crisis creates a change, and all change is a bit frightening to us, there must be an opportunity for adjustment or acceptance of the change. People will adjust to change and crisis at their own pace, and as I like to say, *"In their own elegant style."* This adjustment is very smooth for some but rather difficult and jagged for others. Again, our history of dealing with crises in the past, and our personal genetic makeup and personality will determine how quickly and smoothly we make adjustments to a life crisis in the present.

IV.   Reconstruction/Reconciliation Phase

During this phase, we attempt to make final sense of the crisis we have experienced. This takes time, and each person will make peace in their own special way. As Christians, we hope that people will experience reconciliation and gain an understanding of God's plan and purpose in the midst of the crisis.

There is no magic cure for all the situations pastors/counselors face in their attempt to ease the pain of crisis. There is not one specific winning strategy. Thus, more important than our clinical skill (though greater skills should be sought) or theological understanding (grow in God we must) is our ministry of presence – just being a loving, vulnerable, listening ear for the one in crisis. Being there in a time of need can be the most helpful ministry we can give.

The Bible and Crisis

If one were to take time to read the word of God with the specific goal of determining how many crises occurred throughout the Bible, copious amounts of time would be spent outlining such events. The Bible is filled with change, crazy situations, gross immorality, and tremendous miracles outlining the hand of God in the midst of difficult times. In much of the history of the children of Israel, beginning with Adam and Eve's crisis in the garden and through the Babylonian exile, we see crisis situations coming, being resolved, adjustment being made, and hopefully reconciliation occurring for the better. In fact, one scholar has said that the children of Israel's path throughout history was one of:

1. Walking with God
2. Gross rebellion and rejection of the plans of God and
3. Reconciliation and restoration back to God.

Outlined here is a brief picture of the crisis in the Bible, and how it was resolved for the better.

"The Devil Made Me Do It"

From the very beginning God created all things good. But certainly not all things that we experience throughout our lives are good.

When man sinned in the Garden of Eden, a radical change in the way we operate as people began. In Genesis chapter three, we read the account of the temptation and deception of Eve, Adam's fall into sin and their response when God visited them.

The man and the woman in the Garden had a wonderful, intimate relationship with God the Father. They communed with him every day. They had work to do that was meaningful; and they had dominion over all things that God had created. When the fall came, things changed radically.

Reading in verses 7 to 13 of Genesis 3, we begin to see what things changed because of sin. Sin, in and of itself, is a form of crisis.

In verse seven it says, "[7] Then the eyes of both of them were opened, and they knew that they were naked; and they sewed fig leaves together and made themselves [a]loin coverings.

[8] They heard the sound of the LORD God walking in the garden in the [b]cool of the day, and the man and his wife hid themselves from the presence of the LORD God among the trees of the garden. [9] Then the LORD God called to the man, and said to him, "Where are you?" [10] He said, "I heard the sound of You in the garden, and I was afraid because I was naked; so I hid myself." [11] And He said, "Who told you that you were naked? Have you eaten from the tree of which I commanded you not to eat?" [12] The man said, "The woman whom You gave *to be* with me, she gave me from the tree, and I ate." [13] Then the LORD God said to the woman, "What is this you have done?" And the woman said, "The serpent deceived me, and I ate." (NASB)

As you continue through the chapter, the consequences that came upon mankind because of their sin is presented. Along with it is the great promise of God that one would be sent who would bruise the head of the serpent, one who would ultimately defeat Satan and create for us the opportunity of eternal life through Jesus Christ.

Let's briefly review the crisis and results. First of all, (vs.7) states their eyes were opened, they saw things from an entirely different viewpoint than they had before. Prior to their fall, they saw things from God's perfect perspective.

Because of the fall, they saw their nakedness, their vulnerability. One consequence of crisis, especially if it is self-induced, is a loss of God's perspective of the event. Because of that distorted view, when a crisis comes, regardless of the source of the crisis, we rarely respond according to God's perfect plan.

Adam and Eve immediately attempted to hide themselves because they recognized they were naked. Because of their vulnerability, they attempted to withdraw and to cover themselves from their shame. In crisis, an experience of guilt and shame often accompanies the crisis. Some of this is to be expected if personal sin has brought us into crisis, but attempting to hide and withdraw will not resolve the problem, it will only worsen it.

You will further note that when confronted with the statement, *"Who told you that you were naked?"* Adam responded, *"The woman you put here with me - she gave me some fruit from the tree, and I ate it."* Adam projected the blame and the responsibility for his choice onto his wife, which is a common response to pain. One of the first steps toward growth in any situation is the owning of responsibility. No matter what happens (excepting for victims of child abuse), we are responsible for how we respond. Perhaps we are not responsible for the crisis itself, but we must own responsibility for our response if intervention, healing and relief are to come.

Let's look at God's response. The Lord's response was different from the average parent, really quite unexpected. In the midst of their rebellion and disobedience, God comes to them and asks leading but loving questions designed to give them the opportunity to repent and be healed.

Further, God looked after the protection of his children and gave a promise. In spite of the consequences of our sin, he would make a provision for us, showing us the way to right standing with God. How wonderful is the love and grace of God.

Developmental Crises

Times of Transition

A developmental crisis can best be defined as one that occurs during the normal transition times of life. Those primary transition times that are presented within this book include;

1) Marriage
2) Child-birth
3) Child rearing
4) Career changes and development
5) Mid-life transitions
6) Teenagers
7) Empty nest
8) Senior years

There are many situations that can occur which are not necessarily crises, but times of change, which must be adapted to. Let's define these crisis, or transitions that come in the natural flow of life.

Marriage

For those of us who are or were married[1], we recognize that the ideal or perfect relationship that meets all of our deepest longings and needs is more a fabrication of a romanticized society than a reality of our actual experience. Marriage can be and should be a most exciting and wonderful experience. Yet, in the midst of all the romance and the excitement of a relationship, a marriage takes hard work and dedication to make it successful.

Let's look at some of the dynamics that make up a healthy relationship. The first dynamic we will address is the family of origin. As I say in many seminars, *"If I had never had parents, I'd never be crazy!"* What I mean by that is I have learned how to behave, what to expect, how to respond in certain situations, especially crises; within the context of my family of origin. The experiences, the treatment, the relationship that I had with my mother and father have strongly shaped many of my perceptions of the way I am supposed to be as a husband and father; and what a wife is to be as a woman in relationship with me.

It is fairly easy to see how problematic this could be in real experience, especially if you have an immature couple with vastly different cultural backgrounds and personal deficits.

---

[1] For more on marriage, see Marriage and Family Life: A Christian Perspective by Dr. Stan DeKoven.

The marriage dyad, that is the relationship between the two adults, is the most important part of family life. Conflict within a relationship can be linked many times to the family of origin and unresolved conflicts between the spouse and the family they were raised in.

God intended our marriages to be happy and successful, and to be a model to the body of Christ of the strength of God to create a binding relationship that will last forever. God's plan and ideal is one man, one woman, one lifetime, not divorce, remarriage and all that goes with that. At the same time, we must be clear that these crises can occur just because one gets married, as each party brings their past into their present.

What are some of the possible crises in marriage? What are some of the milestones that you can look forward to in a marriage relationship?

The One Year Wonder

The first year of marriage is by far the most difficult in regards to adjustment. A typical couple will enter a relationship starry-eyed, deaf, dumb, blind, and (often) stupid. They have great hopes that every deficiency within their life, which they have brought into the relationship, will be healed and resolved because of the *"love"* of the spouse.

The reality is that two half people do not make a whole. They are only make two half people trying to struggle together to become whole. It takes two whole people to make each other whole and not one of us fits the bill completely. Because of this, pre-marital counseling is strongly recommended to ensure that problems are resolved before the big plunge.

The Seven Year Itch

Second to the potential problems of the first year of marriage is what we call the "seven year itch." This corresponds to the settling in period, with the only too real responsibilities of child rearing, career, and future. It is about this time that couples turn over in bed, look at each other and wonder," *Who is this person that I'm sleeping with?"* The time has come when they re-evaluate what is important in their life. What do they want to do? Is this the person they want to spend their life with? As often occurs, parallel lives can be the solution, where the husband works ten hour days and occasional weekends to "properly provide" for his growing family, and the wife is worn to a frazzle by her home responsibilities. Often, tensions mount, requiring that a man and woman seek some help to manage their burgeoning loneliness and occasional outburst of stress at each other.

Counseling, focused upon re-evaluation of their core values, a re-affirmation of their covenant, and a new determination to make adjustments to meet each other's needs will help, if they are willing. Simple discussions about the problems (after the initial blame game towards each other) will help to avert a greater crisis.

Other Transitions

After that come the fifteen, twenty-five, and forty year marks which are also times of transition. In these times, we evaluate what is most important in our lives. It is an opportunity to recommit ourselves to our relationship with our spouse.

Child-Birth and Parenting

Although we would not call the birth of a child a crisis, it is still a major cause of stress in many relationships.

Children are a blessing from the Lord; a blessing, requiring commitment and courage. For the average parent, the days and nights of childhood are caressed by pain, fear and worry as to what is going on and whether or not their child's needs will be met. Events and experiences in their young lives may leave deep scars and hurts. Not only is the child's physical life a concern, but his or her psychological and emotional well-being can be wounded. Angry shouts of parents, as well as long periods of tension-filled silence can result in damaging a child's emotional welfare.

Family problems can disrupt a comfortable parent/child relationship. Frequent moves, unemployment, financial hardship, illness, death of a friend or family member, or divorce can dramatically change a happy home into a stressful living situation. The child's sense of value, including his/her self worth, is substantially influenced by what he/she experiences in the family. Anxious, uncomfortable parents cause the children to experience what they perceive to be instability and he or she becomes fearful and loses trust in self and in others. Affection, safety, nurture, and stability are such simple needs. But, if these needs are not met within the first few years of life, scars will remain and the needs may never be fully met.

Some of the crises that can occur within a family when a child is introduced into the home are as follows:

The Crisis of Birth

The process of birth is both exhilarating and exhausting. For a small percentage of women, severe depression, even suicidal/homicidal ideation can accompany the birth process (called post partum depression). Prolonged depression may require medical intervention to ensure the safety and health of mom and child.

Focus of Attention

The wife instinctively focuses her life's attention on the needs of the child. This is natural but at the same time can be taken to an extreme. The primary relationship of the family is that of the marriage. Wives who have not had a positive communicative relationship with their husbands can focus so much of their time and attention on the child they neglect the legitimate needs of their husband.

Fathers in turn may feel neglected and left out. The mother must focus on the needs of the child more than on those of the husband, but insecure husbands can experience jealousy leading to arguments, bitterness, and severe distress.

Bringing a child into the home with 2.00 a.m. feedings, crying fits, need for attention etc. can lead to conflict within a husband and wife relationship.

Couples must be able to come into agreement in regards to the style of discipline and ways of communicating in regards to the child. If our parents spanked, we will tend to want to spank. If they used time out, we would want to use time out. If they were over-indulgent, we would tend to be over-indulgent. Or, we might flip to the other end of the spectrum in rebellion to the way our parents raised us. That is why it is so important for parents to refer to the word of God and to wise counsel. Preferably this happens before they ever have children to find out what is a biblical model of discipline that both can agree to and operate in. Nobody's parents were perfect; therefore, we're not going to be perfect parents. That is a myth within the American society: the myth of perfection. We need to recognize that all we can do is the very best we can and learn to love and discipline our children according to biblical standards.

Conflict within families is inevitable. It is important to recognize that there are two primary needs that all of us require.

To have a sense of:

1. Security and safety
2. Acceptance and love

Security, safety, acceptance, and love: these are primary needs of all people and God intends that we have those needs met. It is not the need that is the real problem, it is the strategies that we utilize to meet the need that can be a problem. If we as parents can create a happy healthy family environment, then we can significantly minimize the problems that our children have within the family relationship.[2]

Teenagers

The teenage years are not truly a crisis, although many critical themes are acted out within the high school years. Adolescence is not a disease, as many parents seem to think. It is a time however, of many changes. Many difficult struggles can occur within the teenage years. It is important to review in brief some of the primary crisis situations that can occur during the adolescent period.

Depression

A primary problem faced by many adolescents is depression. What is depression and how does it develop? Depression is defined as a chronic disturbance of mood that involves a profound sense of sadness, lack of energy, and irritability; both in children and adults. The irritability can especially be found in children. Most adolescents can be very, very moody. We are not talking about the normal "moodiness" of a typical adolescent. This is a long-term mood that is profoundly sad with a lack of energy etc. Some of the symptoms include: poor appetite or overeating, insomnia or hypersomnolence, low energy or fatigue, low self-esteem, poor concentration, difficulty in making decisions, and feelings of despair or hopelessness.

---

[2] For more information on marriage, family, and parenting; see <u>Marriage and Family Life</u> and <u>Parenting on Purpose</u>, by Dr. Stan DeKoven.

What are the causes of depression? There are many. We will name just a few.

1. **Genetic and/or Physical:** Improper diet, lack of exercise, poor rest, low blood sugar, and abuse of alcohol or drugs can cause some of these conditions. Further, there seems to be a genetic predisposition toward depression.

2. **The Family Systems View:** In some families where adolescents become depressed there is an apparent lack of warmth, or a sense of rejection, abandonment, or trauma that has occurred in childhood.

3. **Learned Helplessness:** This is a victim syndrome whereby someone who has been significantly victimized through life will learn to respond in a helpless and hopeless fashion. They develop a sense of inadequacy, which is quite pervasive.

4. **Negative Thinking:** Proverbs, says, "As a man thinks in his heart, so is he." Psychiatrist, Aaron Beck has said that our thinking causes our emotions, not vice versa. If you think badly of self and of the world, if you are critical and condemning, you will tend to be blue or depressed most of the time.

There are other areas that are worth noting including life stresses, anger that is turned against the self, guilt over past sins or problems, etc.

What are the effects of depression? They can be many including psychosomatic illness, poor performance, unhappiness, and masked reactions such as drug involvement, impulsive behavior, including sexual behavior, withdrawal, and ultimately suicide.

Briefly, how do we treat depression? Normally through a combination of talk therapy or counseling, and in some cases, medication is sufficient treatment. The primary focus is to encourage the individual to talk about what is going on in their life and to assist them to change the way they think about their situation. Secondly, it helps to change the environment. Sometimes a change of routine, starting to walk, writing out your feelings, seeking forgiveness, forgiving others, getting involved with other projects and other people's lives can be very important in overcoming depression.

Finally, teach them to find a purpose for living, a meaning beyond themselves. As Christians that should be easy, we have life in God and have been given a purpose in Christ. That is to praise God and to win others to the Lord Jesus Christ.

Career Development and the Crisis of the Loss of a Job

Especially in Western nations and primarily for men, one's career and ability to earn a living is a major source of identity and self-esteem. Much of a man's identity is linked to his career.

The thinking about career begins in early childhood. Children take on certain roles and play games to determine, "What are we going to be when we grow up?" Very few of us grow up to fulfill our childhood fantasies. Work and career goals are important in our self-esteem development and in our overall life script, or plan.

The decision for a career is a tremendous one. The decision made is not always based upon logic, but often upon history or influences of other types. In some cases, the young adult will choose a career in rebellion against the parent for the same primary reasons. In choosing a career, it is best to seek the will of God through wise counsel from those within the body of Christ.

Loss of Job

The loss of a job can be devastating. In the midst of this crisis or transition time, one will feel the gamut of emotions. Most men and women who are made redundant are initially angry at the employer, they experience hurt and abandonment and a sense of being lost, being unsure what to do with one's life. One can even become disgruntled with God, wondering why he has allowed this situation to happen.

In the midst of a crisis it is important to remember the following things:

1. Realize that any career is only temporary. Remember it is your employer's privilege to pay you as a member of the kingdom of heaven.
2. Keep a good family support system. All jobs are tentative, even the most secure.
3. Keep things in proper perspective. Rather than looking at your career as a primary importance in life, see it for what it is: a job. Your primary vocation as a Christian is to make disciples.

   Any loss of a job or a major career change can cause stress, but God can help us in the midst of our loss if we hold on to Him and each other in the body of Christ.

Mid-Life Crisis

For men mid-life transition occurs between the ages of 38 and 45. It is a time when they re-evaluate where they are in their life and what they want to do with the rest of their lives. Most men will take a look back at the previous ten years to judge how successful they have been in comparison to their goals and values. If they have done well, they tend to go through the transition smoothly. If they have not accomplished goals, or feel as if they have been cheated in some way by life, they may experience a sense of failure leading to depression or desperation. Further, men begin to recognize that the joys and strengths of youth are beginning to wane. Thus, you will find men who will run out to buy a sports car, put gold chains around their neck, and try to divorce their wives and find a younger woman in their search for youth and vitality. All this frantic and self-destructive behavior, rooted in selfishness is an attempt to chase away the fear of death. Similar to this transition for men is...

Empty Nest Syndrome

The empty nest syndrome for most women corresponds with men's mid-life transition. It tends to occur when children begin to leave home. This is especially difficult for women who have invested their entire life in the care of their children. It is also difficult if their relationship with their spouse has not been a healthy one. Much of a woman's identity can be wrapped up in the role of "mother". They may forget that their primary responsibility is to their spouse. They can suffer a loss of sense of self, precipitating a crisis. This can include symptoms of depression, anxiety, and other forms of psychological problems.

For men and women, this is a time of evaluation and re-affirmation of our covenant with our spouse. Necessary changes can and should be made with courage.

The Latter Years

The word of God indicates that those with gray hair, men and women in their later years, are to be shown honor or respect. A reason for this respect is the assumption that much wisdom and knowledge has been gained over the years. We need to respect our elders and treat them with love and kindness so that they are able to fulfill their role in the body of Christ.

Situational Crisis

Situational crises are just that, crises that occur too us or by us, but are not necessarily found in a certain developmental stage.

Substance Abuse

What is substance abuse? Drug abuse, which includes alcohol abuse, can be defined as the use of any chemical substance that causes physical, emotional, or social harm to a person or to people close to him or her.[3]

In the United States, the level of drug abuse and alcohol abuse among young people is the highest of any developed country in the world. At the present there is an estimated 3.3 million teenagers who would be classified as alcoholics. Nearly two-thirds of our youth have tried an illicit drug at some time before they graduated from high school. Many children who are into heavy drugs by the age of 17 have started as early as age 11. One-third of all suicides, which we have talked about above, regardless of the age, are alcohol related. National estimates of the annual cost to the United States because of drug abuse and alcoholism are over 100 billion dollars.

What are some of the causes of substance abuse and how can we deal with it?

1. **Family problems.** In a chemically dependent family, members may unknowingly encourage drinking or drug behavior.

What is the intervention that can occur to assist the family?

    a) Intervention is designed to motivate the abuser to seek help. Without help, whether through intervention by the Spirit of God by a tremendous conversion experience, or through the loving support of a family, the abuser is

---

[3] See <u>Substance Abuse Therapy</u> by Dr. Stan DeKoven

likely to continue to abuse drugs as a way to meet their desperate needs.

b) **Treatment, w**hich should include an experience with God, and help from a 12 step program or trained counselor.

c) Along with that, most substance abusers must learn how to re-socialize themselves. In most cases, they have had very little or poor parenting. They need to re-learn how to live their lives in a more appropriate manner.

d) There is certainly no substitute for learning the word of God and applying it to their lives. They need a strict and disciplined approach because they have learned to be very undisciplined and very self-absorbed.

Eating Disorders

There are tremendous pressures placed upon adolescent females to be perfect. The underlying belief is that we cannot be accepted unless we are razor thin, have perfect straight teeth, gorgeous hair, and an IQ of 160. To a teenager, trying to fit in as a part of a peer group is a major need. As a result, women are choosing radical and unhealthy ways to become accepted in a peer group.

What are the eating disorders and the counseling issues related to them?

1. **Bulimia and Anorexia**. These are two bingeing and starving disorders that afflict thousands of adolescent and young adult women. The

characteristics of these disorders and the psychological family profile of the victims are very important and are described here.

a) Bulimia is a recurrent episode of binge eating followed by awareness that the eating pattern is abnormal, with subsequent fear of being unable to stop voluntarily. This is followed by a depressed mood and self-deprecating thoughts of guilt and severe anxiety.

   The majority of bulimics will binge in secret and resort to self-induced vomiting, or purging. A typical binge averages over 4,000 calories, lasts for as much as an hour, and occurs up to twice a day. The damage that is physically done in bulimics is tremendous and therefore there is a great need for medical, as well as psychological and physical care.

b) Anorexia is characterized by a 25% weight loss, or a body weight that is 25% below normal. Anorexics have an intense fear of becoming obese. They suffer from a distorted body image.

The typical person with an eating disorder is often seen as a model child, the perfect little princess. Behind this is a very poor self-image, a need for approval, especially from parents, and a compulsion for high achievement. Most of these adolescents see any form of flaw within their character or body image as a distinct failure, which they assume will invite rejection from those that care about them.

The families of most anorexics and bulimics are dependent on each other and cannot handle stress and anger in a positive way. They are enmeshed, that is they are overly concerned and overly involved in each other's lives. Everybody knows everybody's business. There are no clear boundaries between individuals. Paradoxically, the eating disorder functions to preserve family stability.

How does one deal with this crisis? As with many problems in our lives, you must first confront the denial that exists within the family system.

After confronting the denial, it is important to recognize that this is a family problem, where a multi-disciplinary approach is needed. There must be physical needs met through nutrition and sometimes pervasive medical care, along with individual, family and group counseling. This problem is generally beyond the scope of a lay counselor, but knowledge of the disorder and early intervention with a good referral to a mental health professional can save the day.

Teenage Pregnancy

Teenage pregnancy and parenthood has been a major social issue for many years. Approximately 5% of teenagers become pregnant every year. There are major decisions that must be made during this time of crisis.

What are some of the ways that we can avoid the possibility of teenage pregnancy? First of all, especially with the onset of AIDS and all the problems of socially transmitted diseases, it is important that the church be willing to teach and train their young people to have a healthy biblical view of human sexuality. We should not leave it to our schools or peers to teach our teens about this important topic.

How do we respond if a teenager does become pregnant? As with any crisis, we must face it squarely and hopefully with grace. This is not easy for the parent who experiences the shocking revelation that their daughter is pregnant. We must focus on:

1. The emotional, spiritual and physical needs of the teen that is pregnant.

2. The need to provide acceptance while facing the consequences that lie straight ahead.

3. The importance of beginning the necessary planning for the future without condemnation, which is easier said than done.

Solving the Problem

Although we have most of the knowledge and resources needed to solve the problem of teenage pregnancy, we have failed to do so. Despite the growing public concern and the plethora of reports, there has been little action. The elements of a comprehensive, national program have been put forward, with varying emphases by a number of groups.

Elements of such programs include:

1. Realistic sex education from a Christian perspective.

2. Pregnancy counseling services from a Christian perspective.
3. Adequate prenatal, obstetric and pediatric care and loving ministry for teenage mothers and their children.
4. Educational, employment and social services for adolescent parents.
5. Return to solid Christian family values.

No one program can possibly solve the many problems that are associated with teenage pregnancy. The solution must come from elements of society: parents, the churches, the schools, state and local legislatures and government agencies. Most people agree about the importance of finding solutions and services for teenagers, but there is no one willing to pay the costs for such programs in most communities of the nation.

Suicide

Suicide... The very word sends sharp pains of emotion through those whose lives it has touched. Suicide is always accompanied by the question, "WHY? Did I do something wrong? What could we have done differently?"

A 1984 edition of the Evangel Digest reported that in Katonah, New York, "youth suicides" have reached "National crisis proportions," according to Lt. Gov. Alfredo DelBello. The national suicide rate for 15-24 year olds rose from 8.8% to 11.7% for each 100,000 persons from 1970 to 1983. Last year alone 6,000 young people took their own lives. During the last 30 years, the suicide rate among young people has grown 300%. There were 4.5 suicides per 100,000 youth in 1950, compared to 12.3 per 100,000 in 1980.

When most clients reveal suicidal thoughts to their counselor, they are engulfed in pain and feel desperately alone. They feel disconnected and believe that no one wants to or is able to hear the depths of their pain. Hearing their pain and the unique story surrounding it may give the client a feeling of connection to the counselor. Listening to their pain diffuses the urgency of the suicide and may even have a cathartic value in letting the client ventilate (Callahan, 1998). Each minute spent listening to the client's story takes them another step back from the precipice that is suicide.

The questions that must be answered are:

1. Is the client's level of perturbation high enough to move suicidal ideation into suicidal behavior?

2. Does the client have the resources to overcome the suicidal seduction?

3. Is the client's perception contributing to the choice of death (e.g. hopelessness) or life (e.g. a problem-solving attitude)?

4. What is the lethality of the client's plan of suicidal action?

Hopelessness is a psychological trait that has been closely linked to predicting suicide and Westefeld, et al.

(2000) has evaluated the *Hopelessness Scale* to be a solid measure of hopelessness.

Crisis Intervention

The clinician must consider hospitalization of the client, at least on a short-term basis, even if it is involuntary (Westefeld, et al., 2000). A counselor can create a contract with the client in written form and have it signed by both the client and the counselor. Such contracts typically specify the duration of the contract and specify an alternative plan of action in case the suicidal ideations become overwhelming. Writing contracts is a fairly standard practice in this field. Other important considerations include:

Avoid Panic

To react to a crisis with panic is to lessen your chances of gaining a successful solution.

Avoid Pressure

Pressure lures us to a false sense of security. Often the teen gives in to the pressure to do as we ask, only to continue on in his own way in seclusion.

Avoid Prejudice

Avoid any prejudicing of your interactions with the teen because of the crisis. Don't allow the crisis to cast a dark shadow over your relations with him.

Warning signs:

There are certain signs that mental health experts have isolated as warning signals that may indicate suicidal tendencies. Listed below are some of the most common things to look for.

1. Radical personality changes such as persistent sadness, loss of interest in usual activities, feelings of guilt, worthlessness and helplessness.
2. Impulsive behavior.
3. Inability to tolerate frustrations. This translates into wanting everything here and now.
4. Withdrawal from family, friends and regular activities.
5. Noticeable changes in eating or sleeping habits or energy levels; sometimes he will neglect his personal appearance.
6. Falling grades in school or withdrawal from work and other relationships.
7. Difficulty in concentrating.
8. Violent or rebellious behavior.
9. Drug and alcohol abuse.
10. Physical symptoms often related to emotional disturbances, such as stomach, headache, or fatigue.
11. Thoughts expressed of despair, death or suicide.
12. Suicide attempts, even those that are meant to fail.
13. Verbal hints or statements such as, "I won't be a problem for you much longer."
14. Putting their affairs in order.

15. Suddenly becoming cheerful after prolonged depression, the final decision has been made, which in itself is a form of relief.

16. Feelings of a desire for revenge against a former girlfriend or boyfriend or other offending person.

17. Magical thinking. This clearly signals a break with reality. It is an inability to deal with the pressures and the need to believe in some power outside of himself to bring solutions.

One must understand the cumulative nature of stress and its impact on people. They must admit to the existence of problems when they occur and confront them at the time.

What if it happens to me?

There are some general tips and hints that should help if you feel that a crisis is at hand.

Implement a cautious detailed plan of action. It is crucial to cope with your feelings of panic and frustration. There are three vital things that will help you as a family to deal with the problem.

- ADMIT IT! It does no good to take the "Ostrich Approach" and pretend the problem does not exist.

- TALK ABOUT IT! Even if it is painful, it is very important to TALK!

- WRITE ABOUT IT. Involve all family members. This helps to de-mystify what you are feeling and experiencing at the moment.

The Slap Method

A number of suicidal intervention programs across the country use a method of assessing the degree of risk. It is called SLAP!

SLAP seeks to find out:

S...*Seriousness* of intent. Take every cry for help seriously: it's important to discover as quickly as possible how lethal (intent on dying) the person is. Is he/she experiencing so much pain that he/she could easily make a serious attempt at a moment's notice?

Ask these questions:

1. Have you ever thought of killing yourself before?
2. How often do you think about it?
3. Have you ever tried? When? How?
4. Have you thought of how you might do it this time? (It's fair to assume the more detailed the plan, the higher the risk that is involved).

L...*Lethality* of method. The method of choice gives some indications as to the level of seriousness or desire to die. Obviously, a gun can do far more irreversible damage than a bottle of aspirin. A slit throat is potentially far more serious than a slit wrist. Historically, men have chosen more violent methods than women, but recent reports indicate an increase in violent methods among women. At times, the method of choice is simply governed by what is available. There have been kids so intent on dying that they mangled their arms with a plastic picnic knife because it was all they could get.

A...*Availability* of method. Is the method of choice available? How available is it? The person who is fascinated by ending his or her life with a gun, but doesn't have one, may be at less risk than someone who has decided to use a less violent method but has it available. In deciding the level of risk, we must consider both the method of choice and its availability.

P...*Proximity* to help. The young girl who decides to overdose in an abandoned barn some distance from home or friends should be considered at higher risk than a guy who cuts his wrist in the kitchen when Mom and Dad are in an adjoining room. If a method of choice involves some distance from helping resources (possibility of being discovered), it's of a higher risk.

Although no cry for help should be ignored, the SLAP series of questions should give you a more informed sense of the level of seriousness. You're now prepared to make more intelligent decisions on how you should proceed. The young person who has had a fleeting thought of suicide but has gone no further with it presents far less threat than one who has a clearly imagined plan and intention to die.

Suicide is not an impulsive act but the result of a three-step process:

1. A previous history of problems
2. Problems associated with adolescence
3. A precipitating event

There seems to be universal agreement on the manner in which to counsel suicidal people:

1. Be non-judgmental.

2. Treat the youth's problems seriously, and take all threats seriously.

3. Do not try to talk the person out of it.

4. Ask direct questions, such as, "Have you been thinking of killing yourself?" Don't be afraid that you will be suggesting something that the adolescent has not yet considered; usually your mentioning the topic is a relief.

5. Communicate your concern and support.

6. Offer yourself as a caring listener until professional help can be arranged.

7. Try to evaluate the seriousness of the risk, in order to make the appropriate referral to a health care professional, counselor, or concerned teacher.

8. Do not swear to secrecy. Contact someone who can help the adolescent if he or she will do it personally.

9. Do not leave the person alone if you feel the threat is immediate.

    In a counseling situation, a contract can be an effective prevention technique. Once past the crisis, follow up is crucial because most suicides occur within three months of the beginning of improvement, when the youth has the energy to carry out plans conceived earlier.

Families Coping With Trauma

Since the emergence of PTSD the systemic causes and consequences of trauma have become clear (Figley, 1983m 1989, 1997). Systemic traumatology is concerned with the systemic (e.g., interpersonal and intra-relational) causes and consequences of traumatic events (Figley, 1998, 1999). This is one of the least studied, yet most important, areas within the field of traumatology. It attends, for example, to such questions as the following:

1. How do couples cope with the loss of a child and other tragedies they experience?

2. How and why does family violence exist and cease?

3. How can the intergenerational cycle of violence be ended?

4. How do social support groups, including families, prevent and reduce traumatic stress?

5. How can small work groups and other identifiable systems recover from the death of a co-worker and other traumatic incidents affecting the group?

6. How do schools, companies, neighborhoods, and communities prevent, contribute to, and recover from a traumatic event?

7. What are the roles of professionals in assessing and developing prevention and treatment programs?

Diagnosis & Assessment

Traumatized families can be defined as those who are not effectively coping with a traumatic event or series of events that disrupt normal routines, functions, and characteristics of family life (Figley, 1989, 1997). Families must cope with the impact of traumatic stress on individual family members. A person with PTSD may re-experience the traumatic event many times in flashbacks, memories, dreams, or terrifying thoughts. Anniversaries of the experience, or anything that reminds the person of the experience, may trigger symptoms. Persons with PTSD may also suffer from emotional numbness and disturbed sleep, depression, anxiety, intense guilt, irritability, or outbursts of anger.

The counselor should evaluate the family's coping skills that were in place before the trauma. It is also important to provide psycho education about the normal and expected consequences of events such as the one they have experienced.

Exposure, remembering the forgotten aspects to the traumatic event, is vital in enabling the client to recover. Often clients "can't" remember because they are afraid. The flooding of memories can cause distress, and in many clients, a dissociative reaction. If clients are unable to calm themselves quickly, but are able to avoid or control dissociative reactions, they can be treated for symptom management. Training them in effective visualization techniques can be helpful. It is vital for clients to be responsive to one of many desensitization procedures that will enable them to tolerate recall of highly distressing trauma memories.

Treatment Options

Some important goals in treatment are to:

1. Build rapport and trust among family members

2. Clarify the counselor's role

3. Eliminate unwanted consequences of trauma

4. Build family social supportiveness

5. Develop new rules and skills of family communications

6. Promote self-disclosure and other behaviors that promote healing

7. Recapitulate traumatic events

8. Build a family healing theory

The Family Empowerment Treatment approach comprises five phases:

1. Build a Commitment to Therapeutic Objectives

2. Frame the Problem

   a. Telling the Family's Stories

   b. Promoting New Rules of Communication

      c. Promoting Understanding and Acceptance

      d. Listing Wanted and Unwanted Consequences

      e. Avoiding Victim Blaming

      f. Shifting Attention to the Family

3. Reframe the Problem

4. Develop a Healing Theory

5. Find Closure and Preparedness

How Families Work

A family is not just a collection of individuals, but a system of people who interact with one another. A family unit is just that. Each individual member as they interact, impacts the others in a very significant way. There is no greater or more significant relationship developed in human terms than that within the family.

It is also true that the body of Christ is designed to be a family for the people of God. Most of us who experience a "normal" family upbringing recognize that the best of all parents are far from perfect. Therefore, the needs that we have for significance, acceptance, and approval are not totally met within our family of origin.

When families are not functioning well, the balance of the system, called the homeostatic balance, can be upset. At times, an identified patient can emerge. Many times we see, especially with adolescent families, families with teenage children, that one of the teenagers will begin to act out. Pastors/counselors must be willing to deal with the whole family system.

Throughout the rest of this book, you will see ways in which we will attempt to impact, not just individuals, but the families as well in times of crisis. We will attempt to assist families in resolving life's conflicts and transitioning forward towards ever increasing health.

Financial Crisis

One of the most difficult and stressful areas of marital life is caused by financial mismanagement. There are many questions that a couple needs to ask before marriage. If they are married already, they must come to an agreement to function optimally.

Some of the questions include:

1. Who manages the money?

The answer to this is determined by who managed it in the family of origin of each individual. It is very important to recognize that various talents need to be taken into consideration in determining who should manage limited family resources.

2. What if there is not enough money?

Sometimes it is a reality that there is just not enough money coming in to meet the family's financial needs. This can cause tremendous stress on a family. There are no guarantees that the places we work for will always be there to meet our needs. We do know that God will supply all our needs according to his glorious riches in Christ Jesus (Ph.4:19).

Budgeting and understanding God's principles of financial management are very important. Poor decision making in how to spend money and the use of credit can cause overwhelming stress on a relationship.

The advice of John Wesley seems apropo, "Make all you can, save all you can, give all you can."

Divorce

Much like death, divorce leaves a huge residual of grief and sorrow for all involved. One of the differences between death and divorce is that the corpse is still walking around.

Present statistics indicate that 51.7% of people that married in 1989 were divorced before 1995. A recent survey estimated that more evangelical Christians will end up in divorce courts than for the society as a whole.

It is important for someone who experiences the crisis of divorce to be able to keep things in perspective. There is usually no completely innocent party in a divorce situation. Divorce is a symptom of a very dysfunctional marriage that, usually, has been perking along in a negative way for a number of years. It is important to recognize that there must be forgiveness, healing and restoration, which can come through the grief process. The church must teach on the importance of the marital unit and the strength of marriage on a regular basis. We must combat divorce whenever possible.

Conclusion

The issues addressed in this section are by no means comprehensive. The major crisis issues and transitions have been addressed. In the next section, ministry strategies are developed to counteract the needs created by crisis.

Solutions and Treatment

Solutions to a Crisis Situation

There are several steps that a person can take in order to resolve a crisis situation. In order to solve a crisis you must be willing to face the problem. James 5:16, in many ways talks about the need to face the truth, and the need to change. The concept of a positive confession, that is to deny the reality that you are in a crisis, is not biblical. If you have cancer, that is a tremendous crisis. The reality is that you do have a cancer. To say, *"I do not have cancer"*, would be lying to yourself. You can admit, "*I have cancer.*" At the same time, you can also state, categorically and with great faith, "*By his stripes I am healed.*" That is the positive confession, which can lead to positive results.

Secondly, in dealing with a crisis, counselors are to help the individual to untangle their projection system. That is, you can help them to look at things in a more appropriate way. In the middle of a crisis, perceptions can become clouded, judgment impaired. The crisis counselor can assist the one in crisis to see clearly, and make well informed, judicious decisions.

Third, you want to assist them in expressing their feelings in an appropriate manner, to speak the truth in love. It is essential that the church of Jesus Christ create an atmosphere through pastoral staff and trained lay people, whereby crisis situations can be dealt with in a loving manner, whether developmental or situational.

Grief

I have categorized three primary areas of loss that can occur within our lives as people. Those areas are: loss in the area of relationship, loss in the area of events or situations, and loss in the area of self or personal loss affecting our identity. The first area of concern is relationship losses. These are losses that occur naturally or sometimes catastrophically in the course of our lives.

One primary loss, which can precipitate a crisis is the loss of a friend. Friendships are, for many people, very difficult to come by and are very powerful and important. When you lose a friend, someone that you have been close to for many years; whether through death, separation, or just through time and circumstances, it can be a painful process. Some of us do not do well with saying good-bye to friends when we are going to leave. We avoid saying good-bye, or we deal with it tearfully or aggressively. In some cases, we will have a fight before it is time for one to leave and the other to stay behind. In each case, it is important that we go through a grief process. The grief process is like a rehearsal- we are rehearsing the saying good-bye process to those we love and to our own life when that time comes. It is important that we learn to rehearse well and handle the separation, especially of friends.

The second and the most frequent and devastating loss, are separations between husbands and wives. Separations can be most painful, especially in military families or with business executives. When separations occur for long periods of time, it can place great strain on the spouse and the children, requiring supportive care from a loving community.

When one says good-bye, they do so with the expression of feelings, hopefully with affection and touch. It is natural to experience some fear or belief that this may be the last time seeing each other. This dynamic is important to become aware of.

Another area of loss needing assistance can be the loss of children, when the time comes for them to say good-bye. When the last child finally leaves home, there can be an identity crisis that leads to depression and other psychological problems. Therefore, it is important that parents learn how to say good-bye to their children.

Children are given to us by God for a certain purpose. Our goal as Christians is to raise them in such a way that when they turn eighteen we can comfortably release them back to the Lord. Not that we won't continue to love and care for our children, but we will no longer be responsible for their behavior and spiritual walk. We have to let them go.

When divorce occurs, it is important to work through the feelings of anger, hurt, and bitterness and grieve the loss of the spouse once loved. It can take between eighteen months and two years before most people can really let go of the loss. When this is accomplished, there is freedom and opportunity for new relationships to begin.

For those unable to say good-bye and work through the problems of divorce, who are unable to grieve for the loss of what once was; the tendency to repeat the same patterns over and over again throughout their life is great. It is not the same person they marry again, it is just that the person they marry becomes like their former spouse. People carry the problems of the former relationship into the new one.

There can be no greater sense of loss than divorce or death because they are very similar and painful. In these cases, the easiest type of loss is perhaps sudden abandonment in divorce, or sudden death. It is the long- term destructive nature of an embittered and battling divorce or a long- term painful illness and death that causes so much of the grief and heartache. In either case, it is important that feelings be shared and that you go through the basic grief process that has been outlined later in this book.

Models of Intervention

To follow are two primary models used for crisis intervention. Both can be effective in healing clients in need of hope for their journey.

A model for crisis counseling that is simple and effective is the A.B.C.D. model of crisis intervention.

A - To ACHIEVE a relationship. To achieve a relationship it is important to listen fully to the individual's problem without judgment, and with great empathy. The listening process shows that you care and that you are willing to assist the individual in the time of crisis. There is nothing worse than giving trite clichés or pretending to be interested when you really are not.

B - BOIL down the problem. Most people, when they are in the middle of a crisis have a sense that it is astronomical and overwhelming. They feel hopeless to resolve the conflict that they are involved in. Part of assisting them is to break down the components of the problem into smaller bites. Boil down the problem so that it can be managed one-step at a time.

C - You want to CHALLENGE the individual to take constructive action. Questions can help clarify what can be done, such as "What can I do now? What can I do tomorrow? What is my first step?" It is very important that the individual in the crisis, with your assistance; develops a constructive action plan to meet the need.

D - DEVELOP an ongoing plan of action. One of the things that we must recognize is that in most crises, a one shot type of ministry will not work. There must be an ongoing relationship and an ongoing plan of action, and most of the time it is helpful to write these ideas down. Develop goals that will make a difference.

This model, and the one most accepted in clinical circles, is called the Roberts' Seven Crisis Intervention Model.

The following is taken from Crisis Management & Brief Treatment by Albert R. Roberts:

Crisis Intervention: Roberts' Seven-Stage Model

1. Plan and conduct a thorough assessment (including lethality, dangerousness to self or others, and immediate psychosocial needs).

2. Establish rapport and rapidly establish the relationship (conveying genuine respect for and acceptance of the client, while also offering reassurance and reinforcement that the client, like hundreds of previous clients, can be helped by the counselor).

3. Identify major problem(s). This step includes identifying the "last straw" or precipitating event that led the client to seek help at this time. The clinician should help the client focus on the most important problem by helping the client rank order and prioritize several problems and the harmful or potentially threatening aspect of the number one problem. Catharsis and ventilation of feelings are important as long as the counselor gradually

returns to the central focus: the crisis precipitant or actual crisis event.

4. Deal with feelings and emotions. This stage involves active listing, communicating with warmth and reassurance, non-judgmental statements and validation, and accurate empathetic statements. The person in crisis may well have multiple mood swings throughout the crisis intervention. As a result, nonverbal gestures such as smiling and nodding might be distracting and annoying to the person in acute crisis. Therefore, the author suggests the use of verbal counseling skills when helping the client to explore his or her emotions. These verbal responses include reflecting feelings, restating content, using open-ended questions, summarizing, giving advice, reassurance, interpreting statements, confronting, and using silence.

5. Generate and explore alternatives. Many clients, especially college graduates, have personal insights and problem-solving skills as well as the ability to anticipate the outcomes of certain deliberate actions. However, the client is emotionally distressed and consumed by the aftermath of the crisis episode. It is therefore very useful to have an objective and trained clinician to assist the client in conceptualizing and discussing **adaptive responses** to the crisis. "In cases where the client has little or no personal insights, the clinician needs to take the initiative and suggest more adaptive coping methods" (Roberts, 1990, p.13). During this potentially high productive stage, the counselor/crisis intervener and client collaboratively agree upon appropriate alternative coping methods.

6. Develop and formulate an action plan. Developing and implementing an action plan will ultimately restore cognitive functioning for the client. Many clients have great difficulty mobilizing themselves and following through on an action plan. It is imperative that the client be encouraged and bolstered so that he or she will follow through.

7. Follow-up. Stage seven in crisis intervention should involve an informal agreement or formal appointment between the counselor and client to have another meeting at a designated time, either in person or on the phone, to gauge the client's success in crisis resolution and daily functioning one week, two weeks, or one month later.

The Counseling Process

Micro-Systems vs. Macro-Systems

In looking at the over-all management of crisis, especially within the family unit, it is important to think in terms of two view points. One is a micro-system and the other the macro-system.

Micro-System

Micro-system indicates the actual individual or small group counseling process and techniques that assist people in resolving their conflicts. You deal with the smallest possible unit, the individual in crisis or their family.

Macro-System

Macro-system speaks to the need for the body of Christ to develop services and ministries that will prevent, wherever possible, the crises from occurring or provide for support systems to assist with the management of a crisis.

Helpful Techniques Toward Counseling Resolution

There is a four-pronged approach to counseling for those who have experienced crisis.

1. Face it

It is important to help the individual face the problem straight ahead. This is fairly easy to do in the midst of a crisis, as one cannot help but to see what the crisis is. Part of facing it is taking responsibility in the crisis and with it the obligation to act responsibly towards the crisis.

2. Trace it

Trace the origin of the crisis. What things led up to or precipitated the crisis. You must trace back to the origin. This is where asking questions and allowing the individual to talk openly and freely is essential.

3. Erase it

You want to help them say good-bye to the hurts and problems that have been caused. There are several methods by which you can do this.

　a)　Letter Writing or Keeping a Journal

Many times assisting someone to write out what they feel and think, in the forms of prayers or letters to those who have hurt them, can help them process through the anger or hurt they may be experiencing.

　b)　Role Playing

Assisting the individual talk through their hurts is a very helpful technique. Having the client "play" the parts in the crisis, can create greater awareness of feelings which are blocked. These experiential things can help them move past the denial phase and help them in the grief process.

4. Replace it

To replace it means to assist the client find coping skills that can assist them to better handle their life in general, and crisis for the future. This is an ongoing process, and the church and its teaching should be a great support.

Now I want to outline some Macro-system services that can be helpful in the management of crisis.

1. Home Group Concept of Ministry

The small group fellowship, such is a systematic Bible study, prayer meeting, or support group, helps to meet many needs in the area of loneliness. People that have strong social networks when a crisis occurs are better able to manage it.

2. Local Church Lay Counseling

This may include support groups for assisting those with alcohol and drug abuse problems, adult children of alcoholics, child abuse situations etc. A professional or pastoral counselor as a strong adjunct to the local church ministry can train lay counselors.

3. We Are All Equipped to Minister

It is an inherent responsibility of the local church to teach and train people to do the work of the ministry. Eph. 4:11 and 12 speaks of that very clearly. A part of the teaching and training includes:

a) Teaching people parenting skills
b) Marriage and family relationships
c) Financial management
d) Dealing with issues of death and dying, etc.

Seminars and workshops can be brought to the local church to assist with this training.

Assisting to Rebuild Marriages in Times of Crisis

When a crisis occurs within a marital relationship, there are several steps that one can take to assist in the resolution of the crisis times.

First, there are some immediate concerns to be aware of. We must assess the potential for physical violence within the family. Where physical violence occurs, separation is necessary.

When a crisis is occurring in a marriage, as pastoral care people it is important to seek wisdom from God to know whether to intervene or to wait for them to come and ask for help. There are certain things that are important to keep in mind in ministering to people in times of crisis, especially when working with couples. They include:

1. Emotions

Emotions can run very high. Expect much anger, tears, resentment, and bitterness between the two people. This happens normally whenever two people cannot seem to get along together.

2. Time

All problems take time to develop and all solutions take time to be brought to fruition. First, manage the crisis, realizing it will take time to find solutions to long term marital/family problems.

The role of a counselor in this situation is to open lines of communication that are closed when the crisis comes. Many couples are unable to understand each other. Your role is to act as a translator and mediator between the two.

3. Blame

People will be focusing the blame on their spouse, rather than focusing on the issues of their responsibility in the problem. You must reframe their focus. Some things that are helpful include:

1. Providing an opportunity for a controlled expression of emotions
2. As a counselor, you must remain neutral.
3. Create a forum for them to be able to discuss things openly. Confidentiality is important.
4. Encourage the people to talk with each other not at each other, before God.

There are certain things that one should not say in the midst of a marital or family crisis.

1. It is important to recognize that there are no "villains" or "victims". Do not take sides.
2. Do not assume responsibility for patching up someone's marriage.
3. Do not under estimate the potential for acting out, especially of violence in a domestic quarrel.
4. Be careful of unhealthy attractions, or dependencies, that could form between you and the counselee.

5. Romans 8:1 says that there is no condemnation to those who are in Christ Jesus. Those with fallen marriages or difficult family situations know about their failures and are often loaded down with guilt and shame. Be an encourager, not a judge.

The ministry of crisis counseling is one that must be chosen very carefully. It takes great compassion and patience with wisdom to effectively minister to people who are in times of trouble.

Grief and Loss

[18] "The LORD is near to the brokenhearted And saves those who are [a]crushed in spirit."
(Ps. 34:18 NASB)

Grief is an emotional and physical reaction to a significant personal loss.

The Nature of Grief[4]

No one is immune to grief. Grief comes to everyone and it comes in many different ways. Grief is unique and each of

---

[4] Most of this taken from the book, Grief Relief by Dr. Stab DeKoven

us responds to it in different ways. Much of our response is based on our incorporated belief system, which is... how our parents, church, and other social/cultural setting have taught us to respond. However, there are some common experiences we can draw upon, which help us to know about most forms of grief.

Grief Is Painful

The initial response to grief is that....it hurts! King David experienced intense grief at the loss of his son. Absolom was the love of David's life, and the grief that he experienced is a feeling that is common to us all (2 Sa. 12).

Grief is Directional

Grief moves naturally through several stages to a point where you accept your loss and begin to feel and act like your former self.

Grief is Personal

No one feels grief exactly as you feel it. Your feelings and your circumstances are unique.

Grief Moves Slowly

When a loved one dies, do not act as if nothing has happened. This loss is most difficult and significant. It is important to recognize that this is a natural feeling. Try to keep in mind that grief moves slowly and that a sense of meaning returns slowly. Do not condemn yourself for not meeting some imaginary timetable of how long your "grief" should last.

Grief Includes Mixed Feelings, such as...

1. Grief

The pain and hurt of grief is a most common feeling. Grief may also include other feelings however, such as guilt and hostility, which are sometimes not accepted as normal in our Christian worldview. Yet almost every bereaved person feels some guilt and anger, which might even be directed at God.

2. Hostility/Anger

Have you ever asked, *"Why did this happen to me??"* During grief, a person has a right to feel hostile even if the hostility is directed toward the deceased, toward God, or toward the world in general. This is a transitory response to the tremendous loss being suffered.

The external projection on others of anger can multiply the problem. Sometimes a hostile, grieving person can become unknowingly abusive to others. Forgiveness, and letting go of hostility is needed to resolve your grief.

Grief is Natural and Healthy

Grief is a natural and healthy response to a significant personal loss.

3. Guilt Expresses Itself in Many Ways

Guilt is a problem when it controls or dominates you, or when it blinds you to the possibility of resolving your grief and returning to normal patterns of living. Remember, Jesus died for ALL of our sins.

Some guilt is usually caused when a grieving person feels closed off or set apart from others. They will hurt, and are rightly self-absorbed because they are concerned about taking care of emotional wounds.

It is so important to gain victory over guilt; and because of the death of Christ we can overcome irrational guilt. To do so one must;

> a. Acknowledge the need for forgiveness, either of your "sin," your partner's, or others, and forgive.
>
> h. Forgive self - first express the negative feelings about yourself.
>
> c. Accept the Lord's forgiveness according to the Word of God (1 John 1:9).

Some forms of denial of death of a loved one are natural, particularly in the early stages of grief. Denial becomes a problem when it is prolonged or extreme. An example would be when you would buy an expensive gift for the one who died, weeks after their death.

Denial of death or grief for months and years usually means that the bereaved person is also denying other important aspects of life.

The Stages of Grief

Moving through the grief stages is not automatic. You will move through them in different ways and at a different pace than others.

Stage One: Shock

The first stage of grief is shock. With shock, a kind of numbness envelops you. It is nature's natural insulation, cushioning the blow.

Shock and numbness will not prevent you from doing what you must do. You will act, at least in part, instinctively. Whatever your situation, you will retain the capacity to be rational.

Stage Two: Denial

Usually the stage after shock is denial. You understand intellectually what has happened, but on a deeper level, all of your habits and memories are denying the death or the loss had occurred. Denial may remain in some form for months or years. There is no set schedule for moving through this stage.

Stage Three: Fantasy vs. Reality

The third stage of your transition is a struggle between fantasy and reality. This can actually be seen as a component of denial.

Perhaps you find yourself doing, or wanting to do, things the two of you have always done, such as getting the mail or paying bills together.

Whether you only think of these fantasies or act them out, consider them as transitory. This too shall pass.

Stage Four: Grief as a Release

Sooner or later, you will come to realize that your loss is real. The pain of this reality penetrates to your deepest self. You cry and weep. Your feelings come pouring out like a fountain of sorrow.

You may feel as if you are losing control of your feelings. Do not let this worry you. Since you first learned of the tremendous loss, you have come through many stages. It may have taken hours, days, or weeks, but you have come a long way. All the normal emotions that have been denied now express themselves; it is a release. Let it flow, let it out! This is one of God's ways of cleansing you from the pain.

Do not reject those who try and give you false comfort. Just know that there is good health in releasing your feelings and easing your grief. A grieving person who keeps his feelings inside and delays their release for an extended period may experience some reactions.

Stage Five: Learning to Live with Memories

After you have experienced the flood of grief from the previous stage, the pain of grief begins to ease. You are now emerging from the process to the VICTORY. Grief's slow work is not finished though.

Learning to live with memories is a longer-term task.

Stage Six: Acceptance and Affirmation

You are now beginning to accept the loss and to affirm life. Good memories of the deceased are brought to your mind without stabbing pain, and often with gratitude and pleasure for such recollections. Remember, often the process to victory takes years to complete fully. There is no need to hurry it; grief moves at its own pace. Trust the Holy Spirit to do a good work in you.

> *"6 For I am confident of this very thing, that He who began a good work in you will perfect it until the day of Christ Jesus"* (Philippians. 1:6)

What Do You Say To The Children?

Children know sorrow. Who can say that they suffer less than adults? They have needs that should not be overlooked. But, HOW DO YOU TELL A CHILD THAT SOMEONE HE OR SHE LOVED HAS DIED, or when divorce or another major crisis occurs?

It's difficult, but being straightforward is the best rule. Handled carefully, the truth should be good enough.

Your assurance of love and support is the greatest thing you can do for a grieving child. They should be reminded that the loss of one important relationship of love does not mean the loss of others, including your love. They must be made to know they were in no way to BLAME for the death or loss.

Let the child participate in the family sorrow. If shielded, they may feel rejected as though they do not belong.

Protect the child from unnecessary burdens. Having to put up a false front makes grieving more difficult.

Let the child express his feelings. It is all right for the child to be angry. Do not probe or chastise a child for the expression of anger. Often children are unable to directly express their feelings, and do so through their actions. This is especially seen in a child's play. Being sensitive to what a child may be "saying" by their behavior may be especially beneficial. Let the child share in your progress. As you work through grief, coming to terms with your loss, your child will be helped to do the same. Find some activities you can do together, and share your involvement with friends, family, church, and community.

Kindah Greening in his book <u>7 Tips to Survive a Crisis</u> proposes some keen and helpful events.

1. Face the reality of your facts. Denial is not the way to go.

2. Do something about your problem. Take action. Inaction is fatalism.

3. Avoid the blame syndrome. Don't think the world owes you.

4. Ask for help. To survive you must be practical.

5. Cut your losses. Forgetting those things left behind. This is hard to do. Give yourself permission to let go.

6. Decide to move on.

7. Have faith. Learn to draw on your inner resource of faith.

The Need for Wisdom

Here are five scriptures on wisdom to help in the resolution of crises.

1. **Proverb 9** "[9] *Give instruction to a wise man and he will be still wiser, Teach a righteous man and he will increase his learning.* [10] *The fear of the LORD is the beginning of wisdom And the knowledge of the Holy One is understanding.*"

This Scripture indicates the need to have a pursuit of God. Our primary goal, as we go through life, is to know God in an intimate walk with him. That pursuit of God must be a primary focus.

2. **Proverbs 16:20-23**. "*He who gives attention to the word will find good, And blessed is he who trusts in the LORD* [21] *The wise in heart will be called understanding, And sweetness of speech increases persuasiveness.* [22] *Understanding is a fountain of life to one who has it, But the discipline of fools is folly.* [23] *The heart of the wise instructs his mouth And adds] persuasiveness to his lips.*"

We must have a personal knowledge of God's word. Both in the resolution of crisis as a counselor, and in assisting the individual to resolve their crisis, we must understand what God's plan and purpose is according to his word.

3. **Proverbs 15:8** "[8] *The sacrifice of the wicked is an abomination to the LORD, But the prayer of the upright is His delight."*

This verse talks about a commitment to prayer. The people of God must be a people of prayer.

4. **Proverbs 13:20** ".[20] *He who walks with wise men will be wise, But the companion of fools will suffer harm."*

This verse talks about the need to value fellowship with God's people. The desire to isolate oneself, and to withdraw in the midst of crisis must be resisted. We must help people to recognize that fellowship is absolutely essential for normal spiritual growth, and is vital during times of trouble.

5. **Ecclesiastes 11:6** "[6] *Sow your seed in the morning and do not be idle in the evening, for you do not know whether morning or evening sowing will succeed, or whether both of them alike will be good."*

We are to share God's word in a timely manner. There is a time and a season for everything. When going through a crisis it is hard to see how God might work this for good. As counselors, it is many times difficult to see that as well. Yet, we can trust the promise that God's hand is upon the righteous ones and he will see us through to the end.

I only trust that the crises that you will experience, and the critical situations that you will face as a counselor, will be able to be resolved in Christian love and charity.

The Teaching Ministry
of Dr. Stan DeKoven

Dr. Stan DeKoven conducts seminars and professional workshops, both nationally and internationally, based on his books and extensive experience in Practical Christian Living. He is available for limited engagements at Church Seminars, retreats and conferences. Please visit his website for a complete list of books and seminars or you may contact him at:

Dr. Stan DeKoven, President
Vision International University
Walk in Wisdom Ministries
1672 Main Street, E109
Ramona, Ca. 92065
1-800-9-VISION

www.booksbyvision.com
www.drstandekoven.com

Other helpful books by Dr. DeKoven include:

Journey to Wholeness: Restoration of the Soul

Marriage and Family Life: A Christian Perspective

Grief Relief: Prescriptions for Pain After Significant Loss

On Belay! Introduction to Christian Counseling

Family Violence: Patterns of Destruction

Forty Days to the Promise: A Way Through the Wilderness

I Want To Be Like You, Dad: Breaking Generational Curses

Parenting on Purpose

Crisis Counseling: Help in the Times of Change

From Hurt to Healed

Grace and Truth Twin Towers of the Father's Heart

Living in Freedom: The Abundant Life